Rock 'N L Vol

1. p**ai**d   wait   grain   rain

2. mail   snail   chain   train

3. p**ay**   way   ray

4. say   day   play   may

1. **bee**p   sleep   sheep   bee

2. deep   keep   creep   seed   green

3. m**ea**l   leak   seat   heat

4. read   beak   neat   team

5. clean   beach   eat   peace   please

6. meet   meat   feet   feat

7. see   sea   flee   flea

8. b**e**   he   me   she   we

9. **fie**ld   shield   thief   piece   chief

1. **pie**   tie   dried   lie

2. **why**   my   cry   fly   try   by

3. **mind**   kind   find   blind   wind

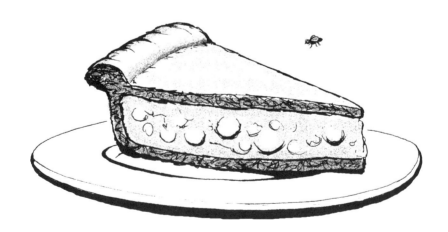

1. b**oa**t   goat   coat   road

2. soap   soak   roast   goal   float

3. t**oe**   hoe   goes

4. **ol**d   hold   cold   sold   told   gold

5. bold   mold   fold   bolt   colt

6. sh**ow**   row   bow   mow

7. low   bowl   grow   snow   blow

8. g**o**   so   no

1. n**ew**   grew   stew   few

2. y**ou**   soup   group

3. fr**ui**t   suit   juice

4. bl**ue**   true   glue   clue

5. flew   flu

6. f**oo**d   boo   mood   zoo

7. cool   tool   fool   pool

8. d**o**   to

1. **car**　far　jar　star　dark　bark

2. sharp　harp　hard　card　barn

3. art　smart　start　part　march

4. h**er**　perk　perch　fern　herd

5. sh**ir**t　dirt　bird　stir　first　third

6. **fur**　curl　turn　burn　hurt

7. blur　purse　curve　burp

8. **for**　porch　corn　or　horn

9. fort　sort　short　sports　born　cord

10. more

(7)

1. **tire**   hire   wire   fire

2. sh**are**   bare   care   scare   spare

   are

3. **air**   pair   fair   hair

★★★★★★★★★★★★★★★★★★★★★★★★★★★★

1. b**oil**   oil   oink   point   coin

2. b**oy**   joy   toy

3. h**ou**se   mouse   out   trout   count

4. south   found   round   our   sour

5. c**ow**   now   plow   how

6. down   brown   owl   crowd

1. **lau**nch   fault   cause   haul

2. dr**aw**   raw   straw   saw   paw

3. **all**   hall   ball   call   fall

4. t**al**k   stalk   walk   salt

★★★★★★★★★★★★★★★★★★★★★★★★★★★

1. person   into   between

2. water   backyard   maybe

3. bedroom   before   remember

4. sunshine   never   upon

5. until   because   myself

6. open   seven

7. **a**bout   away   around   amaze

1. **sing**   ring   thing   bring   swing

2. **ink**   think   stink   shrink   drink

3. th**ank**   sank   blank   drank   bank

4. b**ang**   hang   sang   rang   twang

5. str**ong**   long   song   gong   belong

6. r**ung**   stung   lung   flung   hung

7. ba**dge**   fudge   bridge   judge   hedge

1. la**y**   rainy   tiny   shiny

2. candy   easy   many   any

3. nutty   hobby   puppy   sunny

4. bunny   muddy   foggy   happy

5. piggy   penny   funny   pretty

6. midd**le**   purple   stumble   little

7. tumble   turtle   crumble   bubble

1. steak   break   great

2. bread   thread   head

3. sweat   read   said

4. would   could   should

5. touch   famous

6. shoulder   boulder

7. your   pour   four

8. wood   look   book   roof   good

1. **ph**oto   lau**gh**   phone   cough

2. trophy   tough   enough   elephant

★★★★★★★★★★★★★★★★★★★★★★★★★

1. shoe   most   woman   was   done   been

2. again   both   shall   carry   come   of

3. only   the   does   warm   work   give

4. have   who   once   one   wash   want

5. some   own   put   where   women   they

(13)

1. **sc**ent   scissors   scene

2. **k**now   knot   knee   knew   knock

3. **w**rong   wrist   wreck   wrap   write

4. ri**gh**t   fight   might   flight

5. tight   night   bright   sight

6. sigh   light   high   straight

7. eight   sleigh   weigh   neighbor

8. bought   fought   sought   caught

9. si**g**n   com**b**   thumb   lamb

credits:

Male Vocals: Tom McCain
Female Vocals: Shawn Dady
Long Vowel Rap: D.J.R.J.
Break It Down: Bob Witherspoon

The Phonics Voice: Gabriel Sakakeeny
Male Announcer: Eric Leikam
Female Announcer: Susan Rand
Assistant Announcer: Mick Perry

All instrumental arrangements and performances by
    Brad Caudle.

Illustrations: Bart Harlan
Cover illustration: Christopher Mayes

Page layout by Kathie Caudle and Melissa Caudle.

Special thanks to the many educators who provided
consultation and assisted with field testing.

Recorded and mixed at Spectrum Studios, Houston, Texas.
Remastered at Caudle Brothers Digital, Houston, Texas.

Written and produced by Brad Caudle & Richard Caudle.
©,℗ 1994, 1990 Brad Caudle & Richard Caudle

For additional phonics books, contact your retailer. For the
retailer nearest you, call 1-800-348-8445.